IEBELE ABEL

Episodes

Six piano pieces

EPISODES

Copyright © Iebele Abel, 2021

All rights reserved.

Graphic design by
Studio Hogeland

First edition 2021
Second edition 2024

Printed in the Netherlands

Published by
Elmtree and Waters
www.elmwaters.com

ISBN 9789079735259
BISAC MUS037090

EPISODES

How it is to be born
Watching the emerging dragonfly

Exploratory movements
Water striders making circles in the pond

First love
The mating dance

Building a home
The sparrow collects materials

The hunt
Feeding the young

A natural death
Finding a hidden place to die

There are many behaviors of animals and insects that
are familiar to me. I think we are of the same kind.

Iebele Abel
2021

Episodes

Iebele Abel

1. How it is to be born
Watching the emerging dragonfly

58
63
67
72
p
pp
75
pp
ppp
79

2. Exploratory movements
Water striders making circles in the pond

Iebele Abel

poco allarg.
a tempo
dim.
poco allarg.
a tempo
pp cresc.
p
mp

3. First love
The mating dance

Iebele Abel

11
mf dim.
13
p ppp
15
ppp cresc.
17
mp dim.
p
20
pp cresc.
ppp
cresc.
p

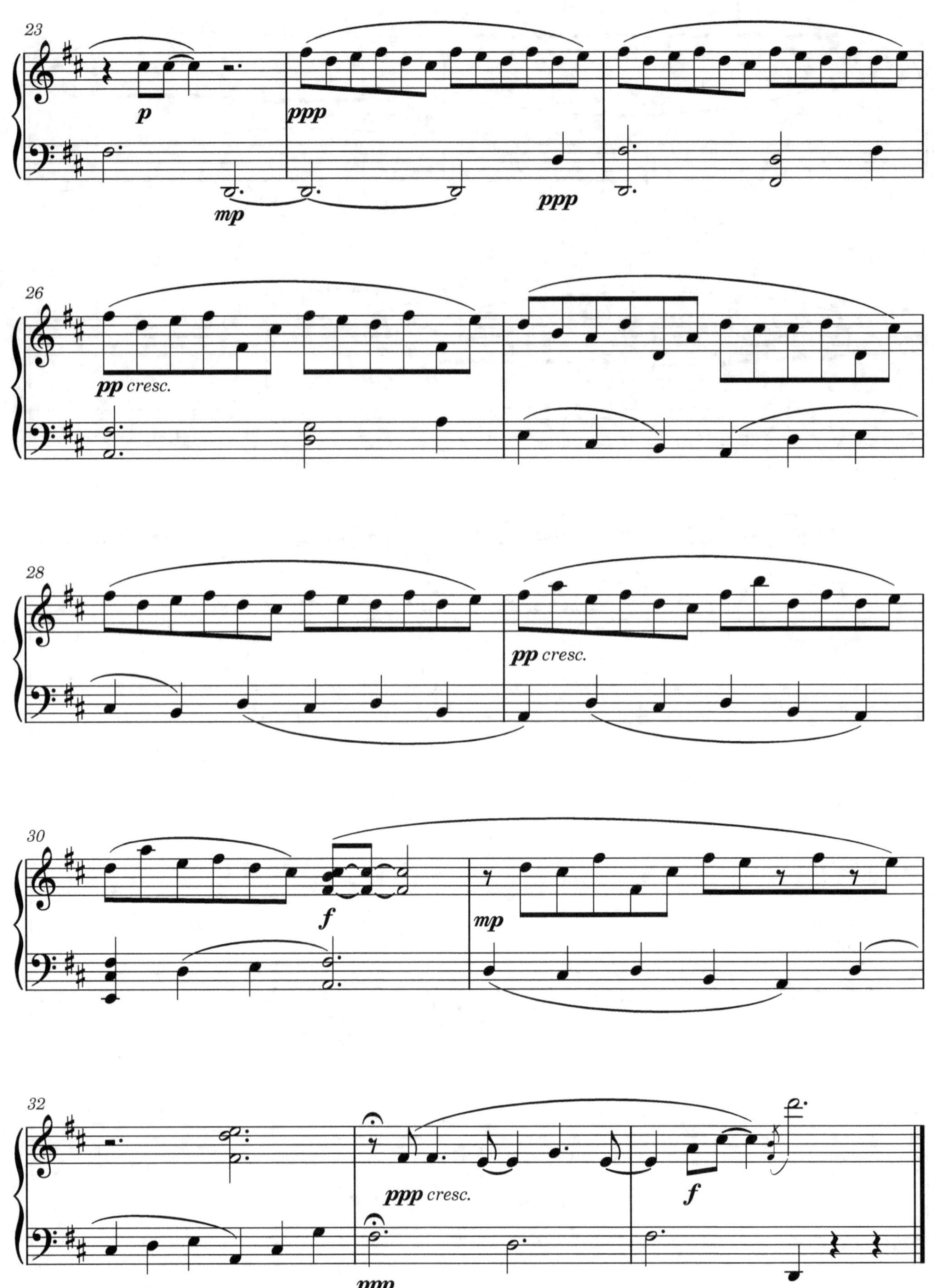
23
p
ppp
mp
ppp
26
pp cresc.
28
pp cresc.
30
f
mp
32
ppp cresc.
f
ppp

4. Building a home
The sparrow collects materials

Iebele Abel

a tempo
p
mp
mf
dim.
f
p

43
dim.
pp
46
cresc.
49
mp
52
ppp
55

5. The Hunt
Feeding the young

Iebele Abel

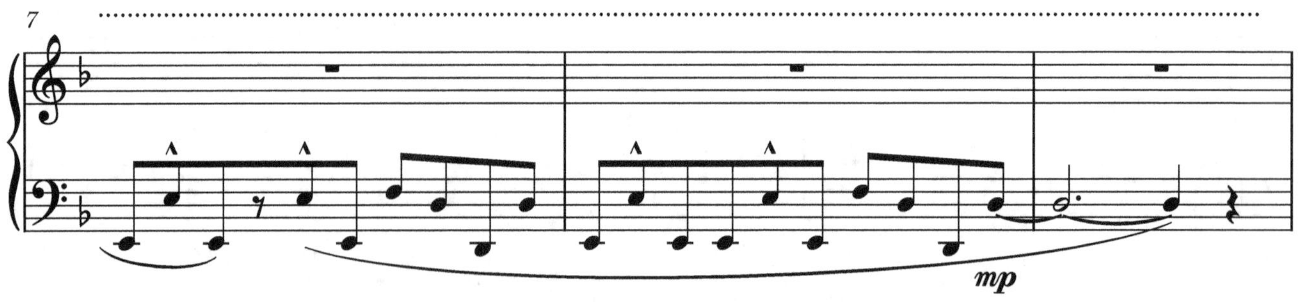

mf dim.
mp cresc.

45
49
55
60
63
66
1.
2.

6. A natural death
Finding a hidden place to die

Iebele Abel

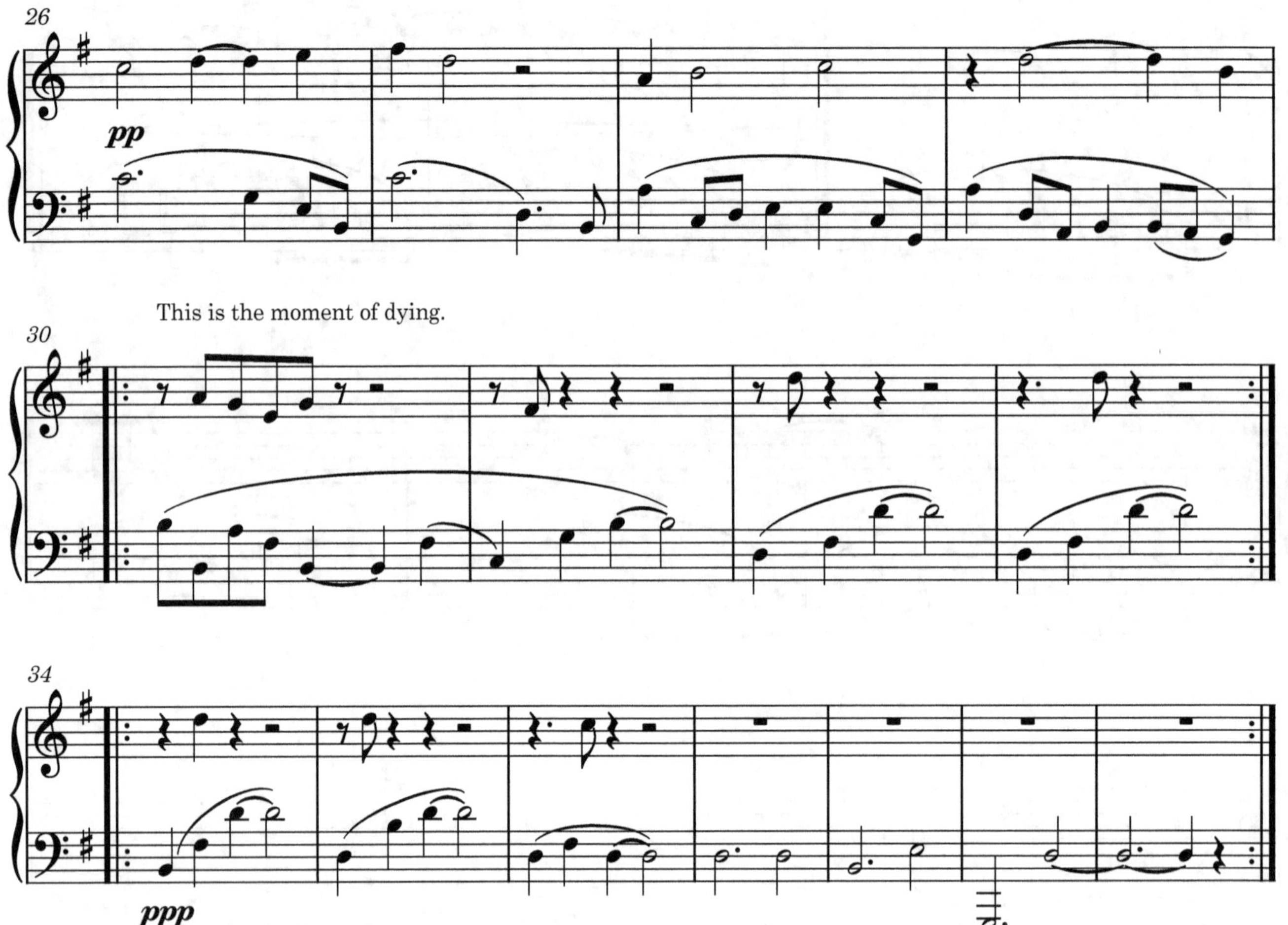
26
pp
This is the moment of dying.
30
34
ppp